from SEA TO SHINING SEA

ARIZONA

By Dennis Brindell Fradin

CONSULTANTS

Harwood P. Hinton, Ph.D., Professor Emeritus of History,
University of Arizona, Tucson

Robert L. Hillerich, Ph.D., Professor Emeritus, Bowling Green State University;
Consultant, Pinellas County Schools, Florida

CHILDREN'S PRESS
A Division of Grolier Publishing
New York London Hong Kong Sydney
Danbury, Connecticut

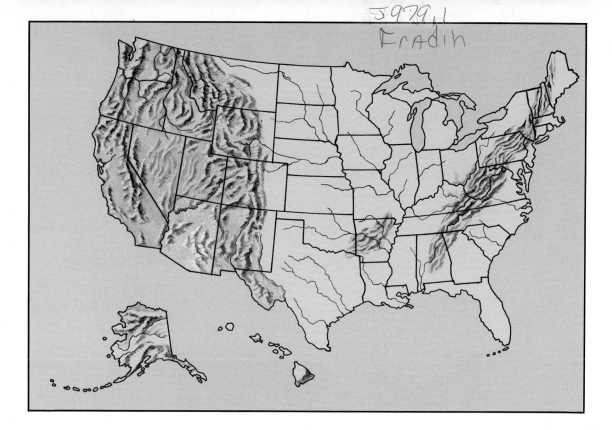

Arizona is one of the four states in the region called the Southwest. The other states in the Southwest are New Mexico, Texas, and Oklahoma.

For Lee and Cyndy Miller

Front cover picture: four mountain peaks east of Phoenix, Tonto National Forest; page 1: Monument Valley; back cover: sand verbena and evening primrose in the desert at Cabeza Prieta National Wildlife Refuge

Project Editor: Joan Downing
Design Director: Karen Kohn
Research Assistant: Judith Bloom Fradin
Typesetting: Graphic Connections, Inc.
Engraving: Liberty Photoengraving

Library of Congress Cataloging-in-Publication Data

Fradin, Dennis B.
  Arizona / by Dennis Brindell Fradin.
   p. cm. — (From sea to shining sea)
  Includes index.
  Summary: Introduces the geography, history, industries, notable sights, and famous people of the Grand Canyon State.
  ISBN 0-516-03803-6
  1. Arizona—Juvenile literature. [1. Arizona.] I. Title. II. Series: Fradin, Dennis B. From sea to shining sea.
F811.3.F69   1993   93-12019
979.1—dc20   CIP
                             AC

Table of Contents

Hopi butterfly dancers

INTRODUCING THE GRAND CANYON STATE

A spring is fresh-flowing water from under the ground.

Arizona is a large state in the southwestern United States. It is a dry land, where water is treasured. The state's name is thought to come from *arizonac*. That is an Indian word meaning "small spring." Arizona's warm weather and Grand Canyon attract many tourists. Arizona's nickname is the "Grand Canyon State."

Arizona has some of the country's oldest Indian ruins. Yet, Arizona is one of the youngest states. There weren't enough people for statehood until 1912. Before that, Arizona was part of the "Wild West." Events such as the Gunfight at the O K Corral took place there.

Today, the Grand Canyon State has one of the fastest-growing populations. Its capital, Phoenix, is one of the country's fastest-growing cities.

The Grand Canyon State is special in other ways. Where do the Cardinals play football and the Suns play basketball? Where was the planet Pluto discovered? Where did Apache leaders Cochise and Geronimo live? Where was the creator of "Sesame Street" born? The answer to these questions is: Arizona!

*A picture map
of Arizona*

*Overleaf: A cholla
cactus field near
Kingman*

"*This Land of Sunshine*"

"This Land of Sunshine"

Arizona covers 114,000 square miles. Only five of the other forty-nine states are larger. Four states and one country border Arizona. New Mexico is to the east. Utah is to the north. Nevada and California are to the west. The country of Mexico is to the south.

Many snow-capped mountains tower 2 miles or more above Arizona. Humphreys Peak is the state's highest point. It stands 12,633 feet, nearly 2.5 miles, high.

Arizona is also known for its canyons, mesas, and deserts. Canyons are deep, steep-sided valleys. The Grand Canyon is the deepest of these. Mesas are flat-topped mountains or hills. Black Mesa and White Mesa are in northeastern Arizona. Deserts are very dry lands. The Sonoran Desert covers most of southwestern Arizona. Arizona's lowest point is in

Arizona touches New Mexico, Colorado, and Utah at the Four Corners. This is the only place in the country where four states touch.

Mesa *is a Spanish word meaning "table."*

Train Rock, in Monument Valley

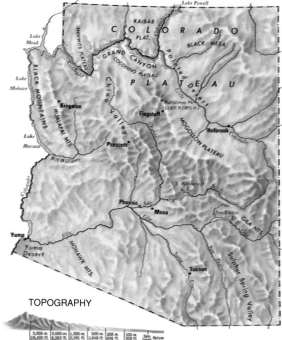

TOPOGRAPHY

the Yuma desert near Yuma. There the land is only 70 feet above sea level.

Above left: Superstition Mountains

CLIMATE

Dunes in Monument Valley

"Come to this land of sunshine," begins "Arizona." That is one of the state's two official songs. Arizona is famous for its warm, sunny weather. Yuma is the country's sunniest city. Skies are blue over Yuma nine out of ten daylight hours.

Winter temperatures of 60 degrees Fahrenheit are typical for Arizona. Summer temperatures often soar above 100 degrees Fahrenheit in the desert.

Arizona is one of the driest states. Its deserts receive only about 2 inches of rain yearly. The

Prickly pear cactus plants in bloom

Lake Mead is the country's largest artificial lake. It covers 250 square miles.

mountains may receive about 30 inches of rain and snow.

WATER, WOODS, AND WILDLIFE

The Colorado is the state's major river. It twists through northwest Arizona. Then it forms most of the state's western border. Other rivers in Arizona include the Gila, the Little Colorado, and the Salt.

In places along Arizona's rivers, dams have been built. Water is stored behind the dams in artificial lakes. Coolidge Dam on the Gila River created San Carlos Lake. Hoover Dam on the Colorado River created Lake Mead. That is at the Nevada-Arizona border. Water from these lakes flows by canal to cities and farms. Without these lakes, many Arizonans would have no water.

One-fourth of Arizona is covered with forests. The state is famous for its ponderosa pines. These 100-foot-tall trees produce fine lumber. Firs, spruce, and cottonwoods also grow in Arizona. The paloverde is the state tree.

Seventy kinds of cactus plants grow in Arizona's deserts. They include the saguaro cactus. This is the country's largest cactus. The saguaro blossom is Arizona's state flower. The "teddy bear" cactus is not cute and cuddly. Its spines can make painful cuts.

Deer are plentiful in Arizona. The ring-tailed cat is the state mammal. It looks like a cat but is in the raccoon family. Peccaries, or javelinas, also live in Arizona. They are strange-looking wild pigs. Bears, elk, mountain lions, and mountain sheep also roam about.

Many animals make their homes in Arizona's deserts. Desert tortoises slowly search for plants to eat. Kangaroo rats jump about on their rear legs. The cactus wren is the state bird. It builds its nest in the cholla cactus. Tarantulas crawl about. Poisonous Gila monsters and rattlesnakes live there, too. The rattlesnake was chosen as Arizona's state reptile.

Mountain lions live in Arizona.

Humphreys Peak, near Flagstaff, is the state's highest point.

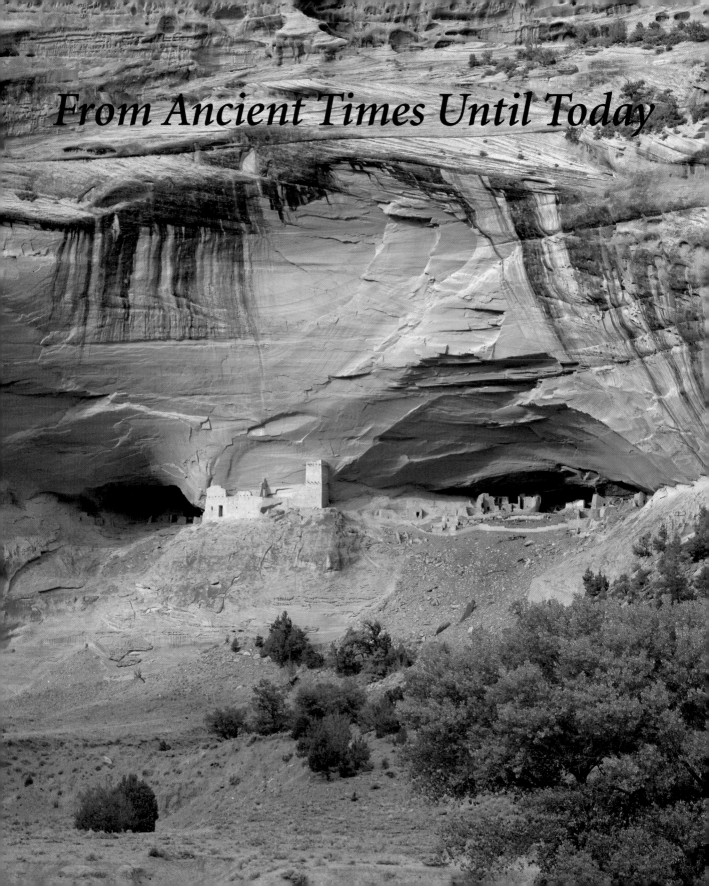
From Ancient Times Until Today

FROM ANCIENT TIMES UNTIL TODAY

Long before there were people, dinosaurs roamed across Arizona. The state has some of the oldest known dinosaur bones. They were found in 1984 in Arizona's Petrified Forest National Park. Those bones date back 225 million years.

AMERICAN INDIANS

Ancient Indians reached Arizona at least 12,000 years ago. These early Indians hunted mastodons. Mastodons were much like the elephants of today. Like dinosaurs, these animals no longer exist.

About 4,000 years ago, the Indians began farming. They grew corn, beans, and squash for food. Farming enabled them to settle in villages.

Arizona's early Indians were great builders. About 2,000 years ago, the Hohokams built canals. The canals carried water to their settlements. The Hohokams also built the Casa Grande. This is a Spanish term meaning "big house." This 40-foot-high building is nearly 700 years old. It stands between Phoenix and Tucson. Casa Grande has

These dinosaur tracks can be seen near Tuba City. They are fossils. Dinosaurs died out about 50 million years ago.

Opposite: Mummy Cave Ruin, Canyon del Muerto, Canyon de Chelly National Monument

Papago women getting water from a well

eleven rooms. It has been called "America's First Skyscraper." About 1,000 years ago, the Anasazis built homes in Arizona's cliffs. Anasazi homes looked much like apartment buildings.

Later tribes were related to these early Indians. The Hopis are thought to be descended from the Anasazis. The Hopis settled in villages called pueblos. They were farming people. Oraibi is a Hopi pueblo in northeast Arizona. It was begun 800 years ago. People still live there. Oraibi is the country's oldest town where people still live. The Hohokams' descendants were the Papago and Pima tribes. They also farmed.

The Apaches and Navajos were closely related tribes. The Apaches lived in the mountains. They traveled on horseback to hunt. They lived in homes called wickiups. The Navajos lived in open country. They hunted and farmed. Their earth-covered wooden homes were called hogans.

SPANISH EXPLORERS AND MISSIONARIES

Many Spaniards came to Mexico in the 1500s. Some came in search of gold and silver. Others came to farm and ranch. Spanish priests hoped to bring Christianity to the Indians.

A Hopi woman making designs on pottery

Indians in Mexico told the Spaniards tall tales. To the north, they said, were wealthy cities. Their streets were paved with gold. The kingdom was called the Seven Cities of Cibola.

In 1539, Fray Marcos de Niza headed north from Mexico. He went searching for the golden land. That year, he became the first known European in Arizona. De Niza saw an Indian village from afar. It was near what is now Zuñi, on the Arizona-New Mexico border. Perhaps the village looked golden in the sunlight. De Niza rushed back to Mexico. He told of seeing one of the golden cities.

Francisco Vásquez de Coronado continued the search. This famous Spanish explorer reached Arizona in 1540. Coronado learned the truth.

There were no golden cities. But some of Coronado's men did explore the Grand Canyon. Coronado left Arizona in 1541. In 1589, Juan de Oñate claimed Arizona for Spain.

SPANISH RULE

During the 1600s and 1700s, Spanish priests came to Arizona. They built church settlements called missions. Father Eusebio Kino came to Arizona in 1692. He began twenty-four missions there. San Xavier del Bac became the most famous. Indians came to the missions. They learned Christianity. Father Kino also taught them new ways of farming.

Father Kino was kind to the Indians. But other missionaries forced Christianity upon them. When silver was discovered in 1736, Spanish miners, ranchers, and farmers came from Mexico. They took the Indians' lands. In 1751, the Indians rebelled against the Spaniards. The next year, Spanish soldiers built a fort at Tubac. It was Arizona's first non-Indian settlement, not counting the missions. In 1776, Tucson was begun as a Spanish fort. Also in that year, the United States declared its independence from England. This new country was far to the east of Arizona.

Spain's grip on Arizona was never strong. Indian uprisings continued. Also, few Spaniards lived in Arizona. By 1820, only about 1,000 Spanish priests, soldiers, and settlers were there.

MEXICAN RULE

Spain ruled Arizona from its colony in Mexico. In 1821, Mexico broke free of Spanish rule. Mexico closed the missions and gained those lands, too. Small numbers of Mexicans continued to move into Arizona. Mexico also let people from the United States enter. Spain had kept the Americans out.

San Xavier del Bac Mission, south of Tucson, was begun by Father Eusebio Kino.

Mountain man Kit Carson

A few American mountain men visited Arizona in the early 1820s. They traveled along the rivers. They searched for beavers. The furs were used to make hats and other clothing. Famed mountain man Kit Carson trapped beavers in Arizona. So did Bill Williams. Bill Williams Mountain and the town of Williams were named for him.

THE UNITED STATES TAKES OVER

The Battle of Vera Cruz took place during the Mexican War.

Many Americans wanted to take land in the Southwest from Mexico. The United States and Mexico went to war in 1846. The United States won the Mexican War in 1848. Through this victory, the United States gained a large part of the

Southwest. All but the southernmost part of Arizona was included. In 1853, the United States bought the rest of Arizona from Mexico. This is called the Gadsden Purchase.

Americans went to Arizona looking for rich mines. In 1854, Arizona's first copper mine was opened. It also produced silver. Gold was found near Fort Yuma in 1858.

As Americans came to Arizona, its two towns grew. By 1858, Tubac had 800 people and Tucson had 600. Soon, Arizona had enough people to be a territory.

In 1863, President Abraham Lincoln signed a bill. It created the Arizona Territory. This was a step toward statehood. Arizona then had a territorial governor and a legislature. Arizonans could also send a delegate to the United States Congress. Charles Poston was the first delegate. He worked very hard for Arizona's causes. Poston is remembered as the "Father of Arizona." But Arizona would have a long wait before becoming a state.

Charles Poston was Arizona's first territorial delegate to the U.S. Congress.

THE ARIZONA TERRITORY

After the Civil War, more people came to the new territory. Farmers planted cotton, grains, and vegetables. They rebuilt and added to the Hohokams' irrigation canals. The city of Phoenix grew around the canals. Ranchers brought in cattle. They hired cowboys to take care of the herds. In 1888, Prescott held the country's first rodeo. Cowboys roped cows and rode bucking broncos for prizes.

Miners found copper, silver, and gold. In 1864, Henry Wickenburg was looking for gold in western Arizona. It is said that he picked up a rock to throw at his stubborn mule. The rock had gold in it. This marked the start of the rich Vulture Mine.

In 1877, Ed Schieffelin went looking for treasure in southeast Arizona. "Instead of a mine, you'll find your tombstone," he was warned. But what Schieffelin found was silver. He named the town that grew up in the area Tombstone.

Other towns sprang up around mining camps. Bisbee, Globe, and Mammoth were three mining towns. These towns were rough places. Gamblers tried to win the miners' and cowboys' money in the saloons. Outlaws tried to steal it. The brothers Wyatt, Virgil, and Morgan Earp worked as lawmen in Tombstone. In 1881, the Earps and "Doc" Holliday faced some cowboys. This was at Tombstone's O K Corral. Six-shooters blazed. Three of the cowboys were killed. Virgil and

Ed Schieffelin made a rich silver strike in Arizona in 1877.

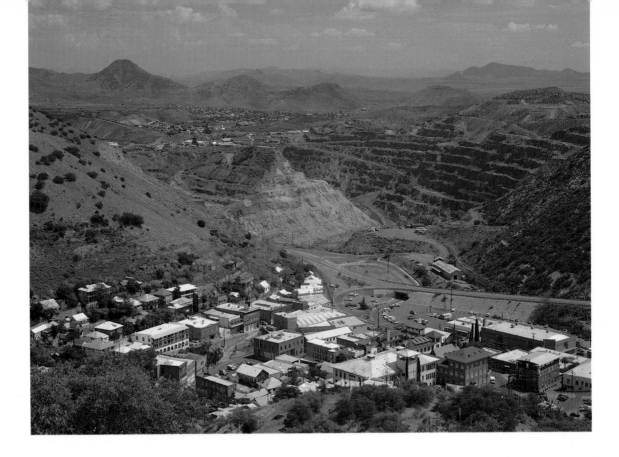

Morgan Earp and Doc Holliday were wounded. This famous event is known as the Gunfight at the O K Corral.

Meanwhile, the Indians were fighting to keep their lands. Apaches under Cochise and Geronimo attacked towns, ranches, and soldiers. In 1862, Cochise and 500 warriors attacked a party of soldiers at Apache Pass. In 1863-64, forces led by Kit Carson captured 7,000 Navajos. This was at Canyon de Chelly.

Cochise's Apaches stopped fighting in 1872. Cochise was about seventy years old. Geronimo sur-

The Lavender Open Pit Copper Mine (above) is important to the old mining town of Bisbee.

rendered in 1886, at Skeleton Canyon. By then, most of Arizona's Indians had been placed on reservations.

During this time, Arizona's population was growing. A railroad reached Arizona in 1877 and crossed the territory in 1881. Trains brought more settlers. By 1900, Arizona's population topped 120,000.

Other territories with fewer people had become states. But Arizona was denied statehood year after year. Many people feared that Arizona was still part of the Wild West. Finally, the long wait ended.

On February 14, 1912, President William Howard Taft signed the bill admitting Arizona to statehood.

Arizona received a Valentine's Day present in 1912. On February 14, 1912, it became the forty-eighth state. George W. P. Hunt was Arizona's first state governor. The capital was Phoenix.

Arizona was called the "Valentine State" at first. As the newest state, it was also called the "Baby State." But the "Grand Canyon State" won out as its main nickname.

World Wars, Dams, and Depression

The United States entered World War I (1914-1918) in 1917. Over a thousand Arizonans enlisted or fought in that war. Mathew Rivers was the first Arizona soldier to die during the war. He was a Pima Indian.

Before and after the war, a network of dams and canals was started. Theodore Roosevelt Dam was completed on the Salt River in 1911. In 1929, Coolidge Dam on the Gila River was opened. Hoover Dam was finished on the Colorado River in 1936. Lakes were created behind the dams. Canals brought water to Arizona's farms, ranches, and growing cities.

In 1919, the Grand Canyon became a national park. Tourism grew in importance to the young

These men were part of the first group of World War I draftees from Arizona.

Theodore Roosevelt Lake and Dam on the Salt River

When the Japanese bombed Pearl Harbor during World War II, the battleship U.S.S. Arizona (above) sank.

state. Hotels and resorts were built to house Arizona's visitors.

During the 1930s, many people passed through Arizona looking for work. They had lost their jobs during the Great Depression (1929-1939). These were years of hard times for the United States. Arizona's farmers and miners also suffered.

World War II (1939-1945) helped end the Great Depression. The United States stayed out of the war for two years. Then, on December 7, 1941, Japan bombed United States ships at Pearl Harbor,

Hawaii. About half the 2,500 people killed were aboard the *Arizona*. That battleship was named for the state. The United States entered the war the next day. Air bases for training pilots opened in Arizona during the war. Arizona cotton went into uniforms. Arizona copper went into weapons. About 36,000 Arizona men and women served in uniform.

GROWTH, PRIDE, AND PROBLEMS

In the 1950s, air conditioning became common in Arizona homes and businesses. This made Arizona's hot summers easier to live through. More people moved to Arizona. Sun City, north of Phoenix, was planned for retired people. Young people with children also moved to Arizona.

As newcomers arrived, Arizona's population soared. There were 749,587 Arizonans in 1950. By 1990, that figure was nearly five times larger—3,665,228. Only Nevada grew faster during that time. Phoenix was one of America's fastest-growing cities during those same forty years. Its population increased ten times what it was in 1950.

The growing state needed more water. The Central Arizona Project was begun in 1974. This

A water-exercise class in Sun City, a retirement community.

big water project began operating in 1985. It brings water by canal from the Colorado River to Phoenix and Tucson.

Arizona wasn't just growing. It was changing. Manufacturing became more important after World War II. Factories sprang up in Phoenix and other Arizona cities. They turned out computers, foods, and many other goods.

Arizona's government leaders were also changing. Lorna Lockwood became chief justice of the Arizona supreme court in 1965. She was the first woman chief justice in the fifty states. In 1981, Sandra Day O'Connor became a United States Supreme Court justice. This Arizonan was the first woman on that court. In 1975, Raul H. Castro became Arizona's first Mexican-American governor. Rose Mofford became its first woman governor in 1988.

Arizona lawmakers and citizens face problems in the 1990s. One problem is widespread poverty. The average Arizonan earns $16,000 a year. This is $3,000 less than the national average. By 1992, 6 of 100 Arizonans didn't have jobs. That's a high jobless rate. Arizona is working to attract more businesses. In that way, more of its people will be able to work and earn a living.

The U.S. Supreme Court is the nation's highest court.

Pollution is another problem in Arizona. Phoenix is working to clean its air. Work is also being done to clean the air over the Grand Canyon. Water management is another problem. The Colorado River has been overused. In 1991, the Colorado was named the country's most endangered river. People use too much of its water. Arizona's groundwater is also in danger of being overused. Arizonans can be fined for using too much groundwater.

Arizonans hope to solve their state's problems by 2012. In that year, the state will be 100 years old. Solving its problems would be a lovely valentine for the Grand Canyon State.

The Colorado River in the Grand Canyon

Overleaf: Gusta Thompson, a San Carlos Apache basket weaver

27

Arizonans and Their Work

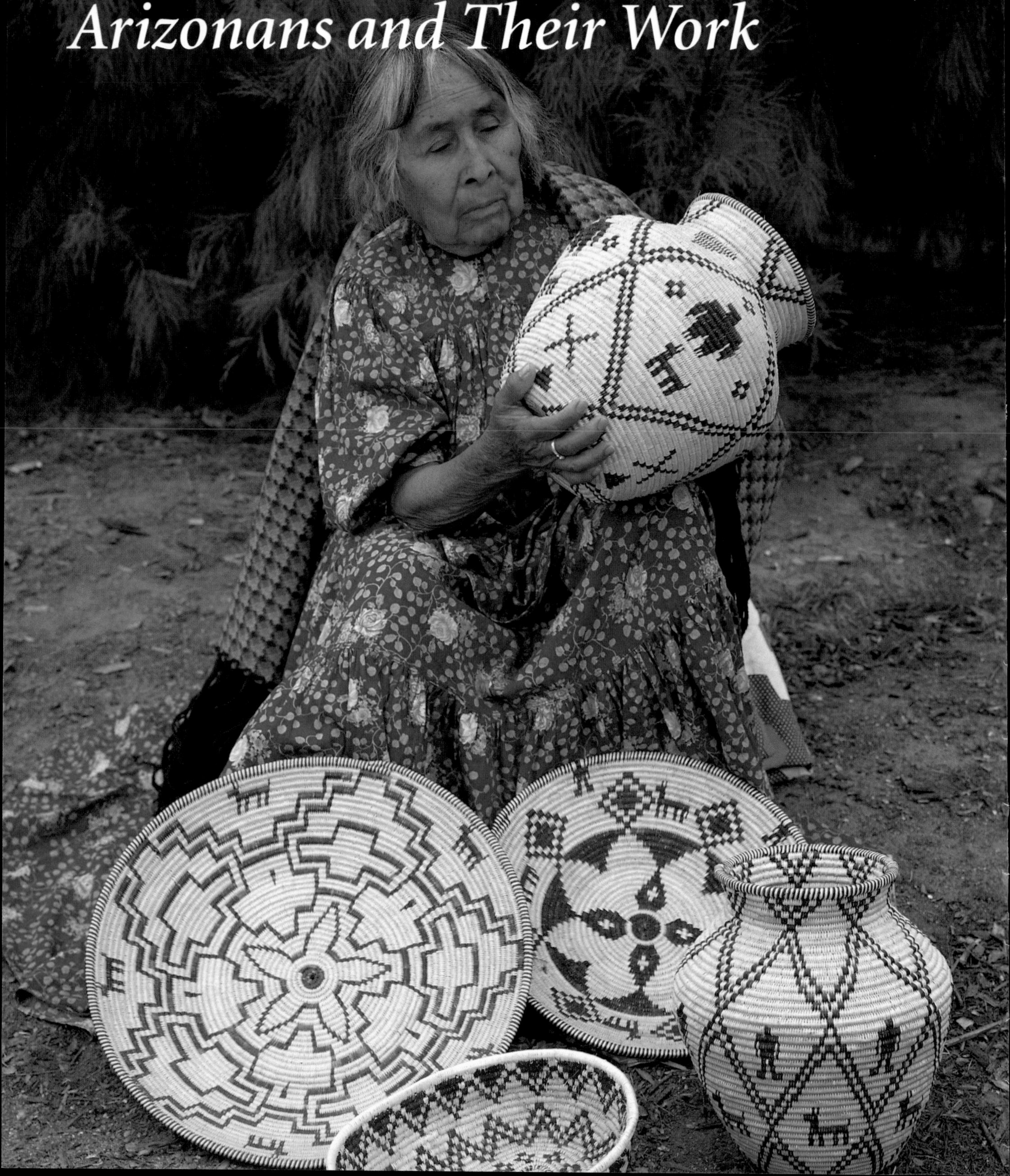

Arizonans and Their Work

The United States Census counted 3,665,228 Arizonans in 1990. The state ranked twenty-fourth of the fifty states in population. Arizona is growing faster than the twenty-three larger states.

Arizona is home to many different kinds of people. About 3 million Arizonans are white. About 700,000 are Hispanic. Only six states have more Hispanic people than Arizona. Hispanic Arizonans hold *fiestas*. This is the Spanish word for "festival." The fiestas are times for dancing, listening to music, and eating delicious foods.

Another 200,000 Arizonans are American Indians. Only California and Oklahoma have more American Indians. A majority of Arizona Indians live on the twenty reservations in the state. Arizona has many places with Indian names. For example, it has Apache, Navajo, and Pima counties.

Arizona's Indians are famous for their crafts. The Navajos weave beautiful wool blankets. The Hopis are known for their kachina dolls. Native Arizonans are also known for making jewelry, pottery, and baskets.

Mexican American children dancing at a fiesta

A Navajo woman in Monument Valley

Arizona also has a growing black population. As of 1990, there were about 110,000 black Americans in Arizona. People from Asia have been the state's fastest-growing group. There are about 60,000 Asian Arizonans. Many of them trace their roots to China, the Philippines, and Japan.

THEIR WORK

Nearly half of all Arizonans—1.5 million people—have jobs. About 400,000 provide services. They include doctors, nurses, and lawyers. People who work in motels and resorts are also service workers. They work in tourism, serving many "snowbirds."

Tourists enjoy rafting and hiking in sunny, warm Arizona.

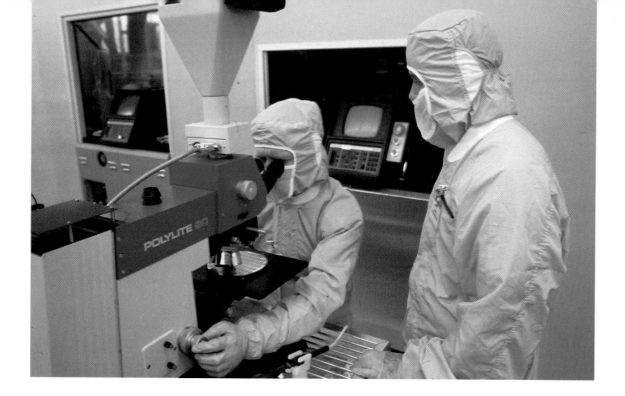

This is what Arizonans call their winter visitors. These people leave their cold, snowy homes for Arizona's sunshine. Tourism is a giant business in the Grand Canyon State.

These workers are making semiconductors for computers.

Nearly 400,000 Arizonans sell goods. They sell such things as Indian crafts and computers. About 250,000 Arizonans work for the government. They work at the state's national parks and seven national forests.

Another 200,000 Arizonans make products. They make airplane parts, auto parts, helicopters, and blimps. Arizona is one of the top ten states at making computers and other office equipment. It also produces golf clubs and tennis balls.

31

Arizona's 40,000 farm workers help feed and clothe the country. Arizona is the fourth-leading state for growing cotton. Cotton is used to make clothing. The state is a leader in raising sheep and horses. Beef cattle are another major Arizona farm product. Arizona grows more lettuce than any state other than California. Arizona is also among the top ten growers of fruits and nuts. They include watermelons, grapes, grapefruit, oranges, pecan nuts, and plums.

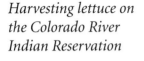

Harvesting lettuce on the Colorado River Indian Reservation

About 12,000 Arizonans work in mining. Arizona is the top copper-mining state. It produces 2 billion pounds of the metal yearly. That is more than the rest of the states combined. United States coins, such as pennies and dimes, contain Arizona copper. The metal also goes into wire, televisions, and pots and pans.

Arizona is a leading miner of molybdenum, gold, and silver. Molybdenum is a metal that is used to strengthen steel. It goes into missiles and airplanes, too. Coal is another major mining product in Arizona.

Coal is a major mining product in Arizona.

Overleaf: A view of the Grand Canyon from the Yavapai Museum

A Trip Through the Grand Canyon State

A Trip Through the Grand Canyon State

About 25 million people visit Arizona yearly. Many visit the Grand Canyon, Indian ruins, and old mining towns. Others play golf, ski, raft, and fish. Still others visit Phoenix and other cities.

The Phoenix Area

Phoenix is the ninth-biggest city in the country.

Phoenix is a good place to start an Arizona trip. Settlers first arrived there in 1867. They saw that Indians had once lived on the site. They named the town for a mythical bird of the ancient Greeks. The phoenix supposedly lived for 500 years. When it died in flames, a new phoenix rose from its ashes. The settlers hoped their Phoenix would rise above the Indian ruins. Their dream came true. Phoenix now has nearly 1 million people. It is Arizona's largest city.

Phoenix has been the Arizona capital since 1889. Visitors can watch lawmakers at work in the state capitol.

Pueblo Grande Ruins is a Phoenix landmark. Hohokam Indians lived there from about 200 B.C.

The state capitol, in Phoenix

to about A.D. 1450. Remains of their canals still exist.

Phoenix also has great museums. The Arizona Museum of History highlights Arizona's early years. The Arizona Hall of Fame spotlights famous Arizonans. The Phoenix Art Museum displays artworks from around the world. The Heard Museum shows southwestern Indian arts and crafts. Many people enjoy the Heard's Hopi kachina dolls.

Besides a Hall of Fame, Phoenix has a Hall of Flame. This museum of fire-fighting equipment is in Papago Park. The Desert Botanical Garden and the Phoenix Zoo are also in the park. The garden has cactuses and other desert plants. The zoo's Arizona

The Hall of Flame is a museum of fire-fighting equipment.

*The pro football
Arizona Cardinals*

*The Arizona Mormon
Temple, in Mesa*

Trail has animals that live in the state. Lizards, coyotes, ring-tailed cats, peccaries, and roadrunners can be seen on the trail.

Sports fans enjoy watching the Arizona Cardinals play pro football. The Phoenix Suns play pro basketball. Many pro baseball teams have spring training near Phoenix. They call themselves the Cactus League.

More than 2 million people live in the Phoenix area. This is more than half the state's people. Six of Arizona's ten largest cities lie just outside Phoenix. They are Mesa, Glendale, Tempe, Scottsdale, Chandler, and Peoria.

Mormons founded Mesa in 1878. This religious group settled the state of Utah. Mesa now has nearly 300,000 people. It is the state's third-largest city.

The Mesa Southwest Museum has exhibits about Mesa's dinosaurs, Indians, and settlers.

Charles Hayden, a trader, began Tempe in 1872. Today, the main branch of Arizona State University (ASU) is in Tempe. ASU has the Center for Meteorite Studies. Meteorites are large rocks from space that sometimes fall to earth.

TUCSON

Tucson is southeast of Phoenix. The name comes from an Indian word. *Tucson* may mean "dark spring." Tucson was founded in 1776 as a Spanish fort. Since then, the city has grown to over 400,000 people. It is now the second biggest city in Arizona.

Tucson is called the "Astronomy Capital of the World." The University of Arizona is in Tucson. That school is helping build the giant Columbus Project telescope. It should be finished by 1997. It will be the country's largest telescope. Kitt Peak National Observatory is southwest of Tucson. The world's largest telescope for studying the sun is there. So is the giant Mayall Telescope. It is used to study distant stars.

A famous movie set is west of Tucson. Called Old Tucson, it looks like the Tucson of the 1860s.

Kitt Peak National Observatory

Old Tucson

The 1939 film *Arizona* was shot there. Many other Western movies and television shows have been filmed there. A western theme park is now at Old Tucson.

OTHER SOUTHERN ARIZONA HIGHLIGHTS

Tourists panning for gold at Old Tucson

Saguaro National Monument is northwest of Tucson. Besides Arizona, the only places saguaro cactuses grow are California and Mexico. A Saguaro National Monument cactus called "Granddaddy" lived 300 years. That is a United States record. Many desert animals eat the saguaro's fruit. The elf owl nests in these tall cactuses. This owl is only 5 inches long.

One of the country's prettiest churches is a short way south of Tucson. This is San Xavier del Bac Mission. The Indians called it "the white dove of the desert."

Southeast of the mission is Tombstone. There, visitors can enter the famous O K Corral. They can also explore Boot Hill. Many outlaws are buried in Boot Hill Cemetery. Tombstone also has Arizona's oldest continuously published newspaper. Its name is the Tombstone *Epitaph.* The words about a person on a tombstone are called an "epitaph." The newspaper's founder supposedly said, "Every tombstone needs its epitaph." Visitors to the newspaper can see early printing presses.

Left: Actors in their roles as the "good guys" at Tombstone. Right: A Boot Hill Cemetery tombstone

Visitors taking a Copper Queen Mine tour

London Bridge, at Lake Havasu City

Bisbee is a famous old copper-mining town. It is just south of Tombstone. Little copper is mined there today. But Bisbee's famous Copper Queen Mine offers tours.

The Papago Reservation is west of Tucson. It touches the Mexican border. The reservation is home to the Tohono O'odham Indians. The name means "desert people." The Tohono O'odham used to be called the Papago. They are known for their pottery and baskets.

Organ Pipe Cactus National Monument is west of the reservation. The organ pipe cactus grows

there. This is the only place in the world where it grows. Its stems look like the pipes of an organ. This cactus grows to be 20 feet tall.

Yuma is in far southwest Arizona. It lies on the Colorado River. Begun in 1854, the town was named for the Yuma Indians. Today, this city of almost 55,000 people is a popular winter resort. Visitors can tour the old Yuma Territorial Prison. It was built by convicts. Many outlaws—men and women—were jailed there. One of the women was Pearl Hart. She held up stagecoaches. The prison museum has a pistol that belonged to her.

ARIZONA'S NORTHERN HALF

Lake Havasu City is in western Arizona. It lies along Lake Havasu. This is an artificial body of water. It was created by Parker Dam on the Colorado River. Lake Havasu City is famous as the home of London Bridge. By the late 1960s, England's London Bridge was falling down. A new London Bridge was built there. In 1968, the old bridge was shipped from England. It took three years to rebuild it in Lake Havasu City.

Prescott is east of Lake Havasu City. Prescott was Arizona's territorial capital (1864-1867 and

The old Yuma Territorial Prison

1872-1889). The territorial governor's mansion can be seen today. It is part of Prescott's Sharlot Hall Museum.

Arizona has many ghost towns. These were once booming mining towns. But people moved away when mining lost importance. Jerome, north of Prescott, almost became a ghost town in the 1950s. Its copper mines closed. Today, Jerome is very much alive. Visitors shop in its many art galleries.

Near Jerome there are remains of ancient Indian towns. Tuzigoot National Monument has 800-year-old Indian dwellings. Montezuma Castle National Monument is also nearby. Indians built this five-story pueblo about 800 years ago.

Northern Arizona's biggest city is Flagstaff. It is north of Montezuma Castle. Settlers first arrived there in 1876. That Fourth of July, they raised an American flag. A pine tree served as their pole, or flagstaff.

Flagstaff is home to Lowell Observatory. From it, Clyde Tombaugh discovered the planet Pluto in 1930.

East of Flagstaff is Meteor Crater. About 50,000 years ago, a 600-million-pound meteor crashed to earth. It left a hole 570 feet deep and nearly a mile across. The dust in the crater is much

Old ore cars at the Douglas Mining Museum in Jerome

July 4, 1876, was the nation's 100th birthday.

like that on the moon. Astronauts train there for moon landings.

Sunset Crater National Monument is north of Flagstaff. A volcano created this hole in the ground. It last erupted nearly 1,000 years ago. Visitors can see a strange light around its rim.

The country's largest Indian reservation covers northeast Arizona. It extends into Utah and New Mexico. The entire Navajo Reservation occupies about 25,000 square miles. Canyon de Chelly National Monument is on the reservation. The monument is an area of red sandstone canyons. Ancient Anasazi cliff dwellings perch in the canyon's walls. Today, Navajo families live in hogans on the canyon floor. Nearby Window Rock is the Navajo

The White House ruin in Canyon de Chelly

headquarters. Each fall, the Navajo Nation Fair is held there.

A colorful desert is also in northeast Arizona. Spaniards named it *El Desierto Pintado*—the "Painted Desert." Sunlight and clouds give the sands and rocks many colors. Dust from the desert even gives the air a pink-purple glow at times. The desert is painted most colorfully as the sun rises or sets. Some colors seen are red, blue, yellow, purple, brown, and pink.

Petrified Forest National Park is in the Painted Desert. Millions of years ago, trees were swept into a swamp there. Minerals in the water entered the wood. After many years, the wood turned to stone.

Left: Petrified Forest National Park
Right: Havasu Falls

One of the world's greatest wonders is the Grand Canyon. The Grand Canyon is in northwest Arizona. The canyon winds for more than 200 miles. It is up to 1 mile deep and nearly 20 miles wide. The Colorado River carved out the Grand Canyon over millions of years. People can drive along the canyon rim. They can also hike or take a mule trip into the canyon.

Part of a Grand Canyon tour includes Havasu Canyon. About 300 Havasupai Indians live on the canyon's floor. *Havasupai* means "people of the blue-green water." The name comes from the water of Havasu Falls.

The Painted Desert

The Grand Canyon is the world's largest canyon on dry land.

A Gallery of Famous Arizonans

A Gallery of Famous Arizonans

Many Arizonans have become famous. They include scientists, lawmakers, and the creator of "Sesame Street." **Geronimo** (1829-1909) was born near Clifton. He was an Apache leader. In 1858, in Mexico, settlers killed Geronimo's mother, wife, and three children. Geronimo then led attacks on white people in Mexico. When he returned to Arizona, he fought the U.S. government. He didn't want the Apaches put on reservations. Geronimo was forced to surrender in 1886. He was imprisoned in Florida for a time. In 1894, he was moved to Oklahoma and became a farmer.

Wyatt Earp (1848-1929) was born in Illinois. He moved West when he was a young man. Earp drove stagecoaches. He also hunted buffalo and worked as a gambler. As a Tombstone lawman, he became a legend. Earp took part in the Gunfight at the O K Corral. He later left Arizona. Earp lived peacefully for many years in California.

Carlos Montezuma (1867-1923) was born in Arizona. As a Yavapai child, Montezuma was captured by Pimas. He was sold to a white man who

Opposite: A painting of Geronimo by Henry Farney

Wyatt Earp

Sharlot Hall

Clyde Tombaugh

gave him an education. Montezuma graduated from the University of Illinois. He then became a famous doctor. He also worked for Indian rights. In the 1920s, he returned to Arizona. He died in a wicki-up on a reservation near Phoenix.

Sharlot Hall (1870-1943) was born in Kansas. Twelve years later, she went to Arizona in a covered wagon. In 1909, Arizona lawmakers made her Arizona's historian. Hall traveled through Arizona to learn about its Indians and pioneers. She then wrote histories of Arizona. The Sharlot Hall Museum in Prescott was named for her.

Astronomer **Percival Lowell** (1855-1916) was born in Massachusetts. He built Lowell Observatory in Flagstaff. The observatory took the first good photos of Mars. In 1905, his staff began searching for a ninth planet. Lowell died before that planet was found.

Clyde Tombaugh continued Lowell's work. Tombaugh was born in Illinois in 1906. He went to work at Lowell Observatory in 1929. Night after night, Tombaugh photographed the sky. He searched the photos for the unknown planet. On February 18, 1930, he spotted the ninth planet in the photos. Tombaugh was only twenty-four when he discovered Pluto.

Carl Hayden (1877-1972) was born in Tempe. His father had founded that city. Hayden served Arizona in the U.S. House of Representatives from 1912 to 1927. He then spent forty-two years in the U.S. Senate (1927-1969). Hayden was ninety-one years old when he retired. His fifty-seven years is the longest anyone ever served in Congress.

Barry Goldwater was born in Phoenix in 1909. He was a World War II pilot. Later, he entered politics. Goldwater was a U.S. senator from Arizona (1953-1965, 1969-1987). In 1964, he ran as a Republican for president. He lost to Lyndon B. Johnson. Many of the Heard Museum's kachina dolls are from his collection.

Stewart Udall was born in Saint Johns, Arizona, in 1920. His brother **Morris Udall** was born there in 1922. Stewart served Arizona in the U.S. House of Representatives (1955-1961). From 1961 to 1969, he was the nation's secretary of the interior. Stewart was in charge of U.S. national parks and other natural resources. Arizonans elected Morris to the U.S. House of Representatives in 1961. He served there for thirty years.

Helen Hull Jacobs was one of Arizona's best athletes. She was born in Globe in 1908. Jacobs became a tennis star. She won the U.S. women's

Carl Hayden

Barry Goldwater

championship four years in a row (1932-1935). Jacobs was the first player to do that.

William Rehnquist was born in Wisconsin in 1924. He was the top student in his class at law school. Rehnquist moved to Phoenix and became a famous lawyer. In 1971, he became the first Arizonan on the U.S. Supreme Court. Rehnquist has been chief justice of the nation's highest court since 1986.

In its first 192 years, the U.S. Supreme Court had 101 judges. All were men. An Arizona woman finally changed that. **Sandra Day O'Connor** was born in Texas in 1930. She grew up on her family's Lazy B Ranch in southeast Arizona. As a child, O'Connor rounded up cattle and drove a tractor. For many years, O'Connor was an Arizona lawmaker and judge. In 1981, she was appointed to the U.S. Supreme Court.

Another Arizona woman helped make learning fun for children. **Joan Ganz Cooney** was born in Phoenix in 1929. She graduated from the University of Arizona. Then she worked as a reporter on the *Arizona Republic*. Later, she worked in television. Cooney thought that television should teach as well as entertain young children. She founded and ran the Children's Television

Joan Ganz Cooney

Each week, 10 million children in the United States view "Sesame Street." The show is also seen in more than eighty other countries.

Workshop. Cooney started the workshop's famous show, "Sesame Street."

Birthplace of Joan Ganz Cooney, Carl Hayden, Geronimo, and Helen Hull Jacobs . . .

Home of Sharlot Hall, Wyatt Earp, and Sandra Day O'Connor . . .

Site of the Grand Canyon, the Painted Desert, and Meteor Crater . . .

The top copper-mining state, and a leader at producing computers, cotton, and sheep . . .

This is Arizona, the Grand Canyon State.

Chief Justice Warren Burger poses with new Justice Sandra Day O'Connor and her family on the steps of the Supreme Court.

Did You Know?

In 1984 a Tucson brother and sister set a world record for growing the biggest known grapefruit. Josh and Allison Sosnow's grapefruit weighed 6.5 pounds.

Big Surf, an amusement park in Tempe, has the world's first and biggest man-made "ocean." Called the Wave Pool, it has 5-foot waves and is about as big as three football fields. People swim and surf at the Wave Pool.

There are many stories about lost gold mines in Arizona. Around 1870, Jacob Walz supposedly found a very rich mine in the Superstition Mountains east of Phoenix. Since he died, many people have searched for this famous Lost Dutchman Mine. Nobody yet has been able to find it.

Arizonans used to tell tall tales about a desert animal called the stick lizard. This imaginary animal was said to carry a stick in its mouth. When the desert grew too hot, it poked the stick into the ground and climbed up. After cooling its feet, the lizard continued its desert journey.

People now buy many items at stores that Indians obtained from desert plants. They used yucca plants to make soap, rope, and sandals. Sap from mesquite shrubs was used as medicine for sore throats. Parts of cactuses provided fruit, wine, water, and even candy.

Tombstone's Rose Tree Inn has the world's largest rose bush. The bush is the size of a basketball court and is more than 100 years old. Each spring it has thousands of tiny white blossoms.

Arizona has towns named Santa Claus and Christmas.

In the 1850s, camels were brought to Arizona and used as pack animals. The camels were later turned loose. They wandered about Arizona for years. The Indians said that one camel turned to rock. That's how Camelback Mountain in Phoenix got its name.

It also has towns called Bumble Bee, Cactus, Grasshopper Junction, Happy Jack, Skull Valley, Snowflake, Sunrise, Sunset, Surprise, and Why.

Harry Mitchell was elected mayor of Tempe in 1978. He taught classes about government at Tempe High School in the mornings and then worked as mayor in the afternoons.

Arizonan Robert H. Starr built the smallest airplane ever flown. *Bumble Bee Two* was less than 9 feet long and weighed only 396 pounds. *Bumble Bee Two* reached speeds of 190 miles per hour. In 1988, it crashed and was destroyed.

The Grand Canyon inspired Ferde Grofé to compose *The Grand Canyon Suite*, a famous musical work.

Arizona Information

State flag

Saguaro cactus blossoms

Cactus wren

Area: 114,000 square miles (the sixth-biggest state)

Greatest Distance North to South: 389 miles

Greatest Distance East to West: 337 miles

Borders: Utah on the north; New Mexico on the east; Mexico to the south and along a small part of the western border; California and Nevada on the west

Highest Point: Humphreys Peak in northern Arizona, 12,633 feet above sea level

Lowest Point: 70 feet above sea level, along the Colorado River near Yuma

Hottest Recorded Temperature: 127°F., at Parker, on July 7, 1905

Coldest Recorded Temperature: -40°F., at Hawley Lake near McNary, on January 7, 1971

Statehood: The forty-eighth state, on February 14, 1912

Origin of Name: *Arizona* is thought to come from *arizonac,* an Indian word meaning "small spring"

Capital: Phoenix (since 1889)

Counties: 15

United States Representatives: 6 (as of 1992)

State Senators: 30

State Representatives: 60

State Songs: "Arizona" by Margaret Rowe Clifford (words) and Maurice Blumenthal (music); and "I Love You Arizona" by Rex Allen, Jr.

State Motto: *Ditat Deus* (Latin, meaning "God Enriches")

Main Nickname: "Grand Canyon State"

Other Nicknames: "Baby State," "Valentine State," "Copper State"

State Seal: Adopted in 1912

State Flag: Adopted in 1917

State Colors: Blue and gold

State Flower: Saguaro cactus blossom

State Bird: Cactus wren

State Tree: Paloverde

State Mammal: Ring-tailed cat

State Reptile: Arizona ridge-nosed rattlesnake

State Fish: Arizona trout

State Amphibian: Arizona tree frog

State Gemstone: Turquoise

State Fossil: Petrified wood

State Neckwear: Bola tie, which was invented in Arizona

Some Rivers: Colorado, Little Colorado, Gila, Salt, Santa Cruz, San Pedro

Some Lakes: San Carlos Lake, Lake Mead, Lake Havasu, Theodore Roosevelt Lake, Lake Powell, Mohave Lake

Wildlife: Deer, ring-tailed cats, bears, elk, mountain lions, mountain sheep, wild pigs known as peccaries or javelinas, coyotes, foxes, porcupines, rabbits, chipmunks, squirrels, desert tortoises, kangaroo rats, cactus wrens, wild turkeys, roadrunners, many other kinds of birds, trout and other fish, tarantulas, Gila monsters, rattlesnakes

Manufactured Products: Airplane parts, helicopters, blimps, auto parts and other transportation equipment, computers and other office equipment, golf clubs and other sporting goods, packaged foods, radios and other electrical equipment, medical instruments, many metal goods, clothing

Farm Products: Cotton, beef cattle, sheep, horses, lettuce, watermelons, grapes, grapefruit, oranges, pecan nuts, plums, milk

Mining: Copper, gold, silver, molybdenum, coal, sand and gravel

Population: 3,665,228, twenty-fourth among the fifty states (1990 U.S. Census Bureau figures)

Major Cities (1990 Census):

Phoenix	983,403	Scottsdale	130,069
Tucson	405,390	Chandler	90,533
Mesa	288,091	Yuma	54,923
Glendale	148,134	Peoria	50,618
Tempe	141,865	Flagstaff	45,857

Ring-tailed cat

Tree frog

Paloverde

Arizona History

10,000 B.C.—Prehistoric Indians reach Arizona

A.D. 1200—The Hopi village of Oraibi (now the country's oldest town) is begun around this time

1539—Fray Marcos de Niza, seeking gold, explores eastern Arizona and claims area for Spain

1540—Spanish explorer Francisco Vásquez de Coronado, also seeking gold, enters Arizona; some of his men explore the Grand Canyon

1692—Father Eusebio Kino begins his mission-building work in southern Arizona

1700—Father Kino begins San Xavier del Bac Mission

1736—Silver is discovered at Arizonac

1752—Tubac, the first non-Indian town in Arizona, is begun as a Spanish fort

1776—Tucson is begun as a Spanish fort; the United States declares its independence from England

1821—Mexico takes control of Arizona from Spain

1848—Most of Arizona comes under U.S. control

1853—With the Gadsden Purchase, the United States gains the rest of Arizona

1854—Copper is found in Arizona

1857—The first stagecoach line crosses Arizona

1859—The *Weekly Arizonian,* the first newspaper in Arizona, is begun at Tubac

1863—The Arizona Territory is created on February 24

1864—Henry Wickenburg opens the Vulture Mine

1867—Phoenix is begun

1870—Arizona's population is 9,658

1872—Chief Cochise stops fighting; his Apaches are later sent to a reservation

A statue of Father Eusebio Kino, in Phoenix

1877—The railroad reaches Arizona; Ed Schieffelin discovers silver in the San Pedro Valley

1879—Tombstone is started near the Schieffelin silver strike

1881—The Gunfight at the O K Corral takes place in Tombstone

1886—Geronimo surrenders, ending the fighting between Indians and Arizona settlers

1889—Phoenix becomes the capital of the Arizona Territory

1900—Arizona's population reaches 122,931

1911—Theodore Roosevelt Dam is completed on the Salt River

1912—On Valentine's Day (February 14) Arizona becomes the forty-eighth state

1917-18—Arizonans help the United States win World War I

1919—Grand Canyon National Park is established

1936—Hoover Dam is finished on the Colorado River

1941-45—After the United States enters World War II, about 36,000 Arizonans serve

1950—Arizona's population reaches 749,587

1965—Arizona's Lorna Lockwood becomes the first woman chief justice of a state supreme court

1974—The Central Arizona Project to bring Colorado River water to Phoenix is begun

1975—Raul H. Castro becomes Arizona's first Mexican-American governor

1981—Arizonan Sandra Day O'Connor becomes the first woman on the U.S. Supreme Court

1985—The Central Arizona Project goes into operation

1988—Governor Evan Mecham is impeached, convicted, and removed from office; Rose Mofford becomes Arizona's first woman governor

1990—Arizona's population is 3,665,228

1994—J. Fife Symington III is reelected governor

1995—Arizona reinstitutes chain gangs in an effort to make prison life tougher

Rose Mofford became Arizona's first woman governor in 1988.

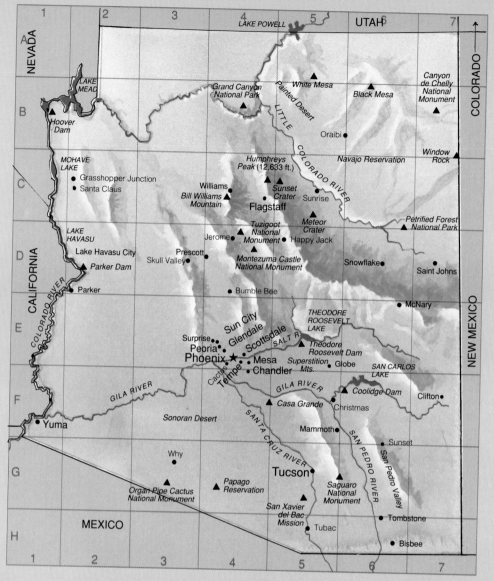

MAP KEY

GLOSSARY

artificial: Made by people; not occurring naturally

billion: A thousand million (1,000,000,000)

cactus: A plant that is known for its ability to live in dry places

canal: A ditch or other artificial structure through which water flows

canyon: A deep, steep-sided valley

capital: The city that is the seat of government

capitol: The building in which the government meets

climate: The typical weather of a region

dam: A structure built on a river to hold back water

desert: A very dry region

dinosaur: A generally huge animal that died out millions of years ago

explorer: A person who visits and studies unknown lands

fossil: The remains of an animal or a plant that lived long ago

Hispanic: A person of Spanish-speaking background

hogan: A Navajo house built of logs and earth

kachina: A Hopi Indian doll

manufacturing: The making of products

mesa: A flat-topped mountain or hill

meteorite: A piece of stone or metal from space that strikes the ground

million: A thousand thousand (1,000,000)

mission: A settlement built around a church

petrified: Turned to stone

phoenix: A mythical bird of the ancient Greeks that rose from its own ashes; the Arizona capital was named for this bird

pollution: The harming or dirtying of the environment

population: The number of people in a place

pueblo: An Indian village built of clay bricks

reservation: Land set aside for American Indians

rodeo: A contest in which cowboys and cowgirls ride horses and rope cattle

saguaro: The largest cactus that grows in the United States

snowbird: The nickname for Arizona's winter visitors, many of whom come from cold, snowy places

spring: Fresh-flowing water from under the ground

territory: Land that is owned by a country but that has its own government

tourism: The business of providing services such as food and lodging for travelers

wickiup: A hut built by the Apaches and other western Indians

PICTURE ACKNOWLEDGMENTS

Front cover, © **Jerry Jacka;** 1, © **Mack & Betty Kelley;** 2, Tom Dunnington; 3, © **Jerry Jacka;** 5, Tom Dunnington; 6-7, © Willard Clay/**Tony Stone Images;** 8, © E. Drifmeyer/**Photri, Inc.;** 9 (top left and bottom), © Tom Till; 9 (top right), Courtesy of Hammond, Incorporated, Maplewood, New Jersey; 10, © Gene Ahrens; 11 (top), © T. Ulrich/ **H. Armstrong Roberts;** 11 (bottom), © Tom Till; 12, © **Jerry Jacka;** 13, © **Jerry Jacka;** 14, **Arizona Historical Society/Tucson #15268;** 15, Arizona Historical Society/Tucson #41964; 17, © **Bob & Suzanne Clemenz;** 18 (top), Arizona Historical Society/Tucson #95; 18 (bottom), **North Wind Picture Archives, hand-colored;** 19, Arizona Historical Society/Tucson #1777; 20, Arizona Historical Society/Tucson #20532; 21, © Tom Hill; 22, **North Wind Picture Archives;** 23 (top), Arizona Historical Society/Tucson #23855; 23 (bottom), © P. Manley/**SuperStock;** 24, **Arizona Historical Society/Tucson #55704;** 25, © **Cameramann International, Ltd.;** 27, © **Jerry Jacka;** 28, © **Jerry Jacka;** 29 (top), © **Jerry Hennen;** 29 (bottom), © **Tom Till;** 30 (both pictures), © **Tom Till;** 31, © **Cameramann International, Ltd.;** 32, © **Jerry Jacka;** 33, © **Barbara Van Cleve/Tony Stone Images;** 34-35, © **Jerry Jacka;** 37 (top), © Jerry Jacka; 37 (bottom), © Mark E. Gibson/**mga/Photri;** 38 (top), © **Jessen Associates;** 38 (bottom), © James Blank/ **Root Resources;** 39, © K. Kummels/**SuperStock;** 40 (top), © Leonard Friend/**N E Stock Photo;** 40 (bottom), © Don & Pat Valenti/**Tony Stone Images;** 41 (left), © John Bramley/**Photofest;** 41 (right), © John Kahle/**Photri, Inc.;** 42 (top), © Mark T. Gibson/**mga/Photri;** 42 (bottom), © **Bob & Suzanne Clemenz;** 43, © S. Maimone/**SuperStock;** 44, © **Bob & Suzanne Clemenz;** 45, © **Tom Till;** 46 (left), © Willard Clay/**Dembinsky Photo Assoc.;** 46 (right), © Ron Goulet/ **Dembinsky Photo Assoc.;** 47, © **Jerry Jacka;** 49, *Geronimo,* painting by Henry Farney, **courtesy of Fenn Galleries, Santa Fe, New Mexico;** 49, Arizona Historical Society/Tucson #1447; 50 (top), **Sharlot Hall Museum;** 50 (bottom), **AP/Wide World Photos;** 51 (top), Arizona Historical Society/Tucson #48722; 51 (bottom), AP/Wide World Photos; 52, AP/Wide World Photos; 53, AP/Wide World Photos; 54 (top), © Jerry Jacka; 54 (bottom), **Arizona Office of Tourism;** 55, **North Wind Picture Archives, hand-colored;** 56 (top), **courtesy Flag Research Center, Winchester Massachusetts 01890;** 56 (middle), © **Jerry Jacka;** 56 (bottom), © Sam Blakesley/**mga/Photri;** 57 (top), © Ruth Cordner/**Root Resources;** 57 (middle), © Meyers/ZEFA/**H. Armstrong Roberts;** 57 (bottom), © Louise K. Broman/ **Root Resources;** 58; © **James P. Rowan;** 59, AP/Wide World Photos; 60, Tom Dunnington; back cover, © Willard Clay/ **Tony Stone Images**

Index

Page numbers in boldface type indicate illustrations.

ABOUT THE AUTHOR

Dennis Brindell Fradin is the author of 150 published children's books. His works for Childrens Press include the Young People's Stories of Our States series, the Disaster! series, and the Thirteen Colonies series. Dennis is married to Judith Bloom Fradin, who taught high-school and college English for many years. She is now Dennis's chief researcher. The Fradins are the parents of two sons, Anthony and Michael, and a daughter, Diana. Dennis graduated from Northwestern University in 1967 with a B.A. in creative writing, and has lived in Evanston, Illinois, since that year.